On the River This Morning

poems by

Barbara de la Cuesta

Finishing Line Press
Georgetown, Kentucky

On the River This Morning

Copyright © 2018 by Barbara de la Cuesta
ISBN 978-1-63534-644-2 First Edition
All rights reserved under International and Pan-American Copyright Conventions. No part of this book may be reproduced in any manner whatsoever without written permission from the publisher, except in the case of brief quotations embodied in critical articles and reviews.

Publisher: Leah Maines
Editor: Christen Kincaid
Cover Art: Watercolor by Marie De Venezia
Author Photo: Paul Dresher
Cover Design: Elizabeth Maines McCleavy

Printed in the USA on acid-free paper.
Order online: www.finishinglinepress.com
also available on amazon.com

Author inquiries and mail orders:
Finishing Line Press
P. O. Box 1626
Georgetown, Kentucky 40324
U. S. A.

Table of Contents

Rivers

On the River This Morning 1

The Cemetery 3

Foreign Parts

Fellow Passengers 9

The Normandie Hotel 12

The Belles Artes

Trompe l'œil 14

The Death of the Peon 16

Life Drawing 17

Prayers

The Shadow Gross National Product

To Sara 25

Markings 27

Monarch 29

We Thought it Would Never End 32

Rivers

ON THE RIVER THIS MORNING

I
On the river, this morning,
a lone egret.
Lone attracts us.

More beautiful and rare
than the many ducks
that lie like stones on the little beach,

Heads under wings.
Their sheeny green necks would be beautiful,
if there weren't so many of them.

II
Today, so still. On the surface a becalmed
 leaf and a duck feather, and deep below
 the cottony clouds.

III
This morning is blustery.
The clouds in their proper place
above the opposite bank.

The marsh grass and the goldenrod
have effloresced into plumes,
The little waves break on the sand.

The long legs of the marsh grass stand
in the tea colored water.

IV
All the berries out today along the river.
Purple gooseberry, red box, cloudy blue juniper,
and flaming bittersweet.

No wind whipping up the river,
only long rolling combers—advancing obliquely
from the little point opposite the harbor—

that intersect and form a soft weave
with another long set coming up the river
from the bay. Sweet and salty waters weaving.

V
The water along the little pebbly beach
is clear the color of a smoky topaz and the plumes
on the marsh grass, silvery toward the coming winter.

This morning is cold
and, after rain, the canvas covers on the boats
are steaming in the sun.

and the tops of the pilings
smoke like chimney pots.

Rain and fog.
Beyond three round buoys, the river,
and the place where I know the point is,
and the docks opposite

And the steeple on the library
All gone
into a pregnant fog,

Nearsighted, I run by the ghostly
Sailboat anchored beyond the motorboats,
and see only the floating debris below:

A styrofoam cup upside down
on leaden water.

VI
A walk on the other side:
Here, the holly and the ivy grow right down
to the bulkhead where the broad furrows comb
the waters from across the river

Where the Admiral Farragut Academy used to be,
and downriver a stilled windmill you never see
but from this vantage,

Above, a wooden porch step with its broken rockers
over turned. The sun sets calmly
and the gulls are silent.

THE CEMETERY

In the 'Seminary' as we called it,
by the Charles River,
we pondered mortality,
among other things.

Near the entry by the railroad bridge
there is a mighty copper beech
all carved with messages,

A sign prohibiting:
Bicycles, Roller skates,
Picnics, Plastic flowers
between April
and October.

We wouldn't have been caught
dead here, on roller skates,
or bringing plastic flowers,
but we did bring sandwiches and
sometimes, bicycles.

The graves begin with some
small markers for the
military dead:

Here Cpl Dennis Ryan received
a musket ball in his leg and died
in 1887.

The Civil War it must have been.
We never knew why
they're buried here.
They weren't local boys.

And, up the hill, the Yankee fathers:
Isaac Watts, the Robert's family:

Mother, Father,
Child dead at fourteen months;
another, eighteen years...

They had a paper mill,
The Roberts family,
where Brandeis is today,

Are gathered within a spiky
iron fence to keep
the rabble out.

Here, Nathanial Weeder,
Engineer, and.
Wife Rebecca
We Will Meet in Heaven...

Sometimes we climbed the
grassy slope
to where the railroad passes,

A Swedish neighborhood.
They came to work
in the watch factory.

Then higher up the French,
the Irish, the Italians,
worked in the mill.

Here the earth is raw.
Like the New Rich,
the New Dead disturb
the neighborhood.

The stones are crisply
chiseled, shiny.

we liked the old ones,
softened by the rain...

But usually,
to avoid the homeless
sitting by the tracks,
we walked below, along the river;

And you
looked under milkweed leaves
for monarch pupae.

Redwings flitted and the
reflection of the old watch factory
wavered in the water.

And we walked out to where
the little spit of land protrudes
into the river,

where we'd lay our bikes down,
sit with our
forbidden sandwiches.

The stone is rough pink marble,
with a plaque attached:

> Anne Hathaway Abbott
> She was above all things
> Glad and Young.

It's at the end of the little point;
the river reeds are just beyond.

Just thirty, when she died we knew
from our subtraction.
Unclear the epitaph.

Shakespeare
I liked to think, led down
a garden path
by Hathaway.

It was actually ee cummings,
I found out many years later, just
as I was about to forget you,

Another friend quoted it at the
top of an infrequent letter.
That's, however,
Another story.

I cut your bangs here
once. Life was so heavy
for you then.

You missed an appointment
at the beauty parlor;
and some occasion
called for grooming.

Your hair was thick and lovely;
You were lovely,
though you wouldn't believe;

A body that refused to hasten after mind;
it tipped a weight that year,

Though previously you had been
glad and young.

I think you wanted then to die,
though still you rode your bike
and clung to most of all the victories

That you'd won the year that you
decided Jesus
was your friend.

You couldn't work,
but painted in bright colors at
the day center where you curled

Back into childhood, and you still
cooked for us sometimes in that
apartment that increasingly reflected
mind's disarray.

Your parents came
a couple times a year to straighten up,
As if that ordering could work
on brain cells.

A problem in the temporal lobe,
The diagnosis, shook you
with violence a day you helped
in kindergarten,

Frightened you that
you might harm
the inconceivable....

But we still had our jokes and ate
our sandwiches by my river.

You always call it, your river,

you objected. It's mine
because I love it, I'd reply.

If it were mine, I'd keep it cleaner,
you. Well, I'm working on it, I.

A great responsibility
to own a river, I.

And we, all of us who loved it,
were pulling mossy supermarket carts
out of its murk, until one day I waded into
its tea colored water, swam a stroke.

You, who earlier
would have followed,
were afraid.

But you liked my flights; and so
I came to own all the places
that we loved, and means of getting there:

The Red Line and the Blue: a futuristic bullet
streaking through its tiled corridors to

WONDERLAND

But my chief possession was the river
and the "Seminary".

And I wonder, sometimes,
did we really ponder, there,
mortality? Not, in any case,
our own…

Your mother wrote four months ago
to say you'd lost your battle as you
waited for another surgery.

You were just fifty, but I think the battle
was half hearted.
You were tired from that
struggle with your body
which began
the day you first

stood up to toddle,
or even earlier.

And I am old and trying to be glad—
It is a duty I have set myself—
and only ponder now,

When I remember sitting by
that uncut gravestone,
lifting up
your heavy hair to cut,

Mortality.

Foreign Parts

FELLOW PASSENGERS

I stow away
car keys, parking ticket
to release me from this lot
in two weeks hence.
so long off, so many perilous
takings off
and landings,
in between this leaving
and return.

The suitcase opened,
fumbled through,
the wait in the long rows

We fellow passengers study
each other, wanting to discover
of late a sign
of a desire to arrive,
return.

Certainly this gentleman opposite
who's carrying an awkward set of
angel wings, this kissing couple,
want to arrive
somewhere.

This woman
with an automatic coffee maker
peeking from a tote,

This group of girls
with tennis rackets…

An elderly man has stumbled
coming up the escalator,
has to be helped to a chair
where his wife cradles his head.

They almost saw it snatched

from them, their trip to Florida,
lost, their next to last,
their last, perhaps…

We all, it's hoped,
want to arrive, to continue
kissing, running after felted balls,
amazing our hosts with the latest
electronic model
of a cook pot.

We board.
The coffeemaker
and the tennis rackets stowed,
the angel wings held carefully
in a father's lap—he plans a first communion
photo, he's explained.

And now the amiable announcements
about the oxygen, the life rafts…
Forced landings at sea are far
from anybody's thoughts these days
along with the quaint fear
of unplanned arrival
in Castro's Havana.

And then the awkward
terrestrial maneuverings of this
winged thing
that gathers speed now
for the thrust that leaves
your stomach behind,

And then, below, the Mullica estuary
And the lacy map of Jersey
coastland unrolled.

I'm seated opposite
the man who fell,
whose wife is wiping
his forehead, these two, gently
aged together, smiling now
tentatively.

The man in the seat next to me

hastens to tell me he's a
divorced dad going to see
his daughter, and I think
 how I've already
divined that somehow
from his face.

He's one of us,
that is to say,
and all of us, it's hoped,
are holding this plane in the air
with our common desire to visit
one more time,

To give our gifts of
angel wings
and coffee makers,
to arrive.

THE NORMANDIE HOTEL
San Juan

It rose up here in San Geronimo
because a San Juan engineer
of legendary wealth desired
a whimsical French woman

On a voyage between the Wars; and later,
when their love ship, painted gray,
a troop ship then, lay aslant
and slowly slipping under mud of
New York harbor,

She had him build her first a floating replica,
a yacht; and, later, this beached tribute: Fourteen decks,
prow turned toward the Fortress of San Geronimo
stern to Isla Verde.

Diminished now by grander vessels,
it is a jewel restored. Art Deco columns line the galleries
that encircle the oval dining hall where white clad waiters
silently set out fruit bowls and clear the decks

For luncheon as I come in to cool myself
from the heat of midday crossing of
the yellow bridge from El Condado
and the broken pavement of the improvised walkway

That skirts the plywood wall which hides
some grand project being carried out involving an

Inversion de $1000000 del Banco Popular

And on which, among the political discourse
and the four lettered bilingual expletives:
Fuck

Is scrawled the love of
Juan Ignacio for his Blanca

I am not lunching, having bought an empanada
from a vendor on the bridge, my hands still greasy.
I come to look at the photos in the gallery
of the French woman in her recreations.

She liked costumes and cavorts here

in gipsy skirts, and here in naval uniform,
or here in toreador pants and spangled shirt.

It is said
that when the Normandie was inaugurated
she scandalized the public bathing naked in its pool.

Also I admire the capitals
of the columns, their stylized
fronds and ocean waves.

Art Deco. An unlikely
English flowering.
Were those precious PreRafaelites having
opium dreams of these tropics,

where floral. fronds and arcs imitate artifice:
the giant hibiscus bowls, the bird of paradise's
reverse curves, the trefoil philodendron,
hieratic ferns, and sword like palms—

I think of Spanish cards,
the cups, the coins, the
swords—that throw their shadow against
a yellow wall?

That sublimate into these capitals
arching like palms over a cool
dining hall where waiters
stand at attention?

Into this love between two wars...?

My hands are greasy and my feet
are burning in their sandals. I take these off
and walk on the Frenchwoman's cool tiles, remembering,
long ago, a child, as my mother tells it,

She was taken through the Holland Tunnel
to see that wartime hulk, heeled over
at its pier before it slipped
beneath the Hudson mud.

The Belles Artes

TROMPE L'OEIL
    Island Heights, N.J.

Retired from the gaudy road to Seaside,
these shady streets of longnecked, Methodist maidens
craning up to catch a glimpse of estuary.

Their lace petticoats showing under eaves,
and round the wide verandahs, rocker crowded,
facing riverward.

Here, his tricky brush employed.
This dark red house with shingle fancywork.
The holly and the ivy crowd his door
with its enamel nameplate: John Frederick Peto.

Uncannily he could reproduce it
at the bottom of his canvas, tempting
outstretched hand to touch.

Come in.
The sunlight through the tinted panes
picks out the china pitchers, rusty horsehoes,
fire irons, bellows hung from beams, a stringless
violin, a pair of candlesticks
above a door, a ragdoll on a sofa.

All this stilled life.

Where's the battered
Cup
We all
Raced for?

Are those thirsty children hiding
down a gloomy corridor?
Whoever bumped
this table, tilting crazily a candlestick,
and causing these books to topple almost…?

Who tore this yellowed notice from a weathered
hoarding? Set up this poor display of pickle jars

and penny barley sticks, toy horse? And slipped
from its moorings a bit this numberplate
revealing a coat
of cheesy yellow paint beneath?

A trick, you say, but there are
Presences, behind a door, or up
a darkened stair. The holly scrabbles
at the colored panes, the stealthy sun
projects a lemon and a cherry lozenge
on the wall.

And here a note's been left
scratched on a yellowed envelope.
Something important inside.
Something important
 behind here
somewhere.

THE LIBERATION OF THE PEON
Diego Rivera

They form a circle round him and
round are the guerilla's faces
and the sombreros, round.
Circlets of bullets crisscross their chests
and pistols ride on hefty buttocks
Round and wild are the horses' eyes
and a lasso holds them
earthbound.

They cover the clay colored
body on the ground
with a ruddy blanket
No *Ascención del Señor de Orgaz* here,

But only a return to earth
under the red petal
of a blanket.

LIFE DRAWING

They all have stories.

There's Debbie, who lives in her van, and believes she can make a living at this modeling business. She's vastly overweight and can't manage any of the athletic poses most of them attempt. But her bulk offers some fine volumes. And Liz so at home in her lush body, her breasts hang like ripe fruit. She has a shop in Belmar sells beautiful scarves. She'll bring one sometime, wrap her shoulders. And the nudist who tells them about his hikes in state parks, wearing just his boots. And the acrobatic Mare, who is an actress at the Repertory, lives alone with her cat, Purple. There's something of a cat in her.

Some Hilda can't see into.

Like the cop with his soldierly poses. She's no idea why he pursues this extra income.

Though doesn't think he's a show off Like some of the men who can hardly control their erections.

Once, bored with his poses, she I saucily blurted out,

"Could you do a fetal position?" Then waited to be arrested, but he meekly complied;

A nice man.

Or that couple…

They came from Perth Amboy, an ugly older man and a tiny woman with exquisite South Asian features. She couldn't help seeing them as a pimp and his woman. They never came back and let themselves be known further.

Phyllis, who runs the group has to go pretty far afield sometimes to find these people and some of her forays are disasters.

Then there is this one up here today Skip, in the Indian underwear he promised to wear. Like Liz, he's at home in his flesh. Apricot skinned in summer, lying on his side, the Indian underwear a bit of a disappointment, but gracefully folded away to reveal his rosy penis cradled in its nest of curly reddish hair, calm as its master.

He has a long curly beard that only we and other intimates know about.
At work and in public he keeps it hidden in his shirt.

We know a lot about Skip because, like his beard, he reveals himself to us. The promised Indian underwear comes from a city in India where he was building a house.

The first time he was in India it was with Mother Theresa.

He was rather scruffy looking back then. We took him for a hippy, but never speculated further.

When he went back to India to build his house, we had a farewell party for him. Potluck.

In the old studio upstairs. All the old timers present. Many dead now.

Then he was away for a more than a year. We thought that was the last of him. But he was back again.

He's meditating she can see. Little smile on his face. She draws him levitated, About a foot above the platform.

Hod...
That house in India never got built. It was the drains
Hod...
One of the names of G-d
The drains had become a Byzantine problem, that drained him.
Like the problems at the Tivoli farm... That Catholic Worker agricultural folly...
Hod...
He's facing the double window. And beyond the wavery old glass the river twinkles, and a sailboat comes into view.
Hod,
Means splendor...

While they study at him and he half listens to them.
Hal Stacy, the retired art teacher and that kind tall woman, Jane, murmur about their arthritis.
This Vioxx, she says. I read the labels always. One of the side effects is sudden death.
Hod...
They all do have shocking side effects, he knows.
I've about a thousand dollar's worth of pills in my pocketbook. But I'm going to throw them out, says Jane.
No, no, give them to me. My God... says Stacy.
Hod...
Hal Stacy is drawing his usual competent contour of Skip's body with a Rapidograph today.
He's the best draftsman of them, and, though retired from his teaching job, still likes to instruct. "Think of your line as an ant crawling over the contours finding where they intersect," he'll tell you if you ask.
Skip shifts his eyes to the line from his hip to his toes, imagines an ant...
Tall, kind Jane is doing him in watery water color on a piece of silk stretched on an embroidery ring.
She reaches for her pocketbook and hands over the sudden death stash hesitantly.
I don't want you to die...
Hal Stacy laughs.
Silence.
Hod...
He loves these people.
There was a fight last week over the young newcomer, Tom, bringing in the electric pencil sharpener and shattering them with its grinding.
Phyllis, had to intervene. Now he keeps it in the back room.
Sometimes Phyllis tells them she thinks she's back teaching kindergarten. She is a benign dictator who's been doing this for twenty years.
Hod.

The drains.
At the Tivoli Farm it was the bedbugs.
Out the window the sail boat crosses the panes, another enters…
Hod… Splendor

At most, Hilda knows he abandoned the plan to build the house in India. She has no idea why.
He returned, but then he left again.
To get a doctorate in nursing. A doctorate! Was there such a thing?
Another farewell party.
No one begrudged him.
Now he's back, with his degree, runs an addiction clinic. It took awhile, he told them. When you go from a degree in philosophy to one in science, you basically have to start right over.
Much less scruffy looking. Sleek in fact. Drives a better car.

Break here.
The electric pencil sharpener grinds in the back room.
Hilda in the kitchen, takes a knife out of the silverware drawer and sharpens the carpenter's pencil she likes to use, holding it over the garbage pail.
Quieter, she thinks, and works perfectly well. Carpenter's pencils don't fit into sharpeners.
She's one of the crochety elders.
Takes coffee, throws it out. Someone must have made it at dawn. Or maybe it's yesterday's.
Tall kind Jane is urging Stacy to give back the pills.
I don't want to think I killed you, she says.
She's quite upset, and he is laughing.
Best deal I ever made, says Hal Stacy.

Skip, stretching his limbs, stands out on the porch, looks at the river and sips the mate tea he's brought from home.
He loves these people. Their brave pursuit of this difficult skill, their frank study of his body, Even if he's given a view of Skip's asshole, Hal Stacy never shifts right or left for a better view.
If he leaves again they'll throw a party for him. Potluck, In the shabby old studio upstairs.

A new pose.

The Thinker. Sitting on a low stool, chin on fist on knee.
Hilda emulates Stacy's contour line. Finding the crossing points. Like a knot, she thinks of certain poses like this. Such a pleasure. The beard and the Indian underwear entwined like a subplot.

Hod.
He spent a year reading Aristotle, Kant, Hegel. Kierkegaard freed him a bit. Then Buber. A philosophy is something you must live.
At Theresa's hospital he learned to touch people. Theresa wasn't a rigorous thinker, But Dorothy was.
Hod…

They really don't know all of this one's story, Hilda thinks.
She recalls a day she spent by herself in the old Seattle Museum, visiting her brother.
An old building, in an overgrown park, given over to statues of the Buddha, once the new museum downtown was built. Her brother dropped her off, and wouldn't be coming back for three hours. Their parent was dying in a nearby hospital.
There must have been at least sixty of them. Buddhas.
She had hours free, so, in spite of them being so similar, she looked carefully at each one and read the little explanatory card.
Learned they were not all Buddhas, some were bodhisattvas.
Reincarnations of the Buddha.
A nice idea.

Hod…
Starting over In the sciences took a lot of his years. You really need several lives, but he's a believer in reincarnation.

She remembers her pleasure at the final Buddha.
Enlightenment, it was called.
The knot undone. The limbs opening up. The mouth open.
And thought how she had earned this pleasure by looking at all the waiting, unmoving, others.

New pose.
He unknots himself, arranges some pillows, lies on his side
Hod
In a way Buber led back to Aristotle, to Aquinas.
It hadn't all been a waste.
Nothing is a waste.
Zaney wants a baby.
Zaney is his girlfriend.
Hod
Something in him resists this.
She won't wait
She can't. He knows.
The first sailboat has disappeared from view.

They all wonder why he doesn't marry Zaney. She's so beautiful and so gentle. Sometimes when they are flush with money, a real treat, they have a pair of models. The cop comes with his wife. But the most thrilling is when Skip brings Zaney.

She can't wait. He knows.
    Hod.
    But he can't either.
    A baby…
    There's that old notion bred in him. That old notion. The mother thing.
    The mother thing that entered Dorothy Day after the abortion, brought about Tamar, and
The Church.
    To menstruate, to conceive in his own body, to swell with life, to labor, to lactate.
    Not that he'd touch his male body.
    Encourage breasts, cut things off.
    He likes to think of seahorses.
    With seahorses, the female delivers the egg to the male, and the male bears the offspring.

Almost feminine, his body, she thinks. Such soft contours, manly contours, but soft, padded, like those Buddhas. A soft reddish fur covers his limbs.
    She couldn't see him as one of those altered people Phyllis brought from Lakewood that time she was desperate for models.
    The carpenter's pencil didn't know what to make of them.

Last pose
    Upright, he wraps himself around his hiking stick.
    A thick maple limb found on the bike trail in Allaire.
    And thinks of his stocks.
    Nutanex
    Anaplys
    Gentex
    That upward slope on CNBC. That climbing zig he watches every morning.
down a bit today, a zag, but for a year now zigging back up that slope
    Hod
    Wiping out his college loan.
    Nutanex
    Anaplys
    Hod
    Make your requests be known.
    Saint Paul.
    Hod.
    He's close lately with his parents. Helped them settle in an adult community.
    Close enough to finally ask his mother,
    Why?

Why, when he was young she hardly ever touched him.
Oh, dear, she said.
It was a book I read.
It wasn't supposed to be good for babies way back when…
Boy babies.
A book my mother…dated even then. I read Dr. Spock when your sister came seven years later…
Is that why you went to India, she asks now, touching his cheek.
I shouldn't have believed that book.
He didn't need to explain to her his other mothers,
Theresa and Dorothy, or mostly Dorothy's daughter Tamar,.
He learned to touch disease and death. It had been necessary.
Dorothy's daughter, Tamar, with her spinning, her weaving, her digging, her planting…
Together they saw the beginning of depression, defeat.
While the Real Depression his parents saw, was a time of exaltation and victory for Dorothy Day.
Hod
"Martyrs are the people who live with saints," Tamar said once.
The alcoholism. The drains, the bugs.
But you can treat depression, alcoholism. Fix drains,
Can't you?
He asked Tamar.
Hod
Still those earlier days were splendid. You had to have that passion for anything to happen.
Lay your requests before God.
Saint Paul.
Now both sailboats are gone.
Nutanex is his favorite.
Go forth. Climb…
The seed of his clinic. His clinic. His Stockbridge. But free to the poor and soiled.
Messy and maternal. But with a rigor… A Benedictine rigor
He is a seahorse. The seed and the egg in one body.
Hod.
Splendor.

Hilda feels compelled to raise his standing figure. Hiking stick, Indian underwear, and all,
just slightly above the platform.

Prayers

THE SHADOW GROSS NATIONAL PRODUCT

Where does it all go?
Sonatas memorized
Clarinet lessons
Sixteen years' worth
Thirty years of
Diaries kept faithfully
Novels in drawers
Out of print
Foreign travel
Photos of
Sketchbooks filled
With long ago nudes, and
Poems on napkins and in
Albums
Painful letters
Initials carved in trees—ah these
last longest—
Chemistry notes
Separations negotiated
Or excruciatingly ripped away
Like bandages from wounds…?

The town dump
You say
Or senescent memory
Or more sentimentally
In memory of friends
Descendants…

Not what I mean
I mean the exquisite learning
Such efforts
Such efforts are said
To alter synapses but
Synapses short circuit don't they
Blow out
In that final effort?

But no
It must

I say

All be preserved
Somewhere
In the germ plasma
I say
In the sub atomic particles
I say

Awaiting confirmation
From cosmologists
Biologists
They
Are my Theologians.

TO SARA

There is a space.
between the atoms,
between electrons,
A space they move in.

Even in this solid pier
on which I sit,
once living wood.

In the densest rock—
though these you do not find,
here in New Jersey's sandy tailing off.

And in that space,
is it, that the dry bones are said
to put on flesh, that the god intrudes
and fecundates?

It is important.
It is important because of you,
longing, like that other Sarah,
like Rachel, like Hannah.

You have had—legs up on stainless steel,
under exquisite clarity of light, even here,
even here the god intrudes—
an embryo implanted.

Seed, I think,
of Mercedes who daily took
the Host, at dawn,
then lay in bed
with Spanish cards laid out,

Playing *tute*
with Alicia Bustamantes

and smoking your
black tobacco
Piel Rojas, betting piles
of dried red beans
you later change for pesos.

Who saw sometimes
into those spaces,.

and made awful and sometimes

beneficent
predictions.

Of Carlos Vicente,
who improbably put a railroad
over those Andes
where you, Sara, came to be born.
and who followed Spengler down a path
of cosmic pessimism.

Or of Gaylord,
named for that ancestor
who carried a church from New Haven
To the cornfields of Nebraska. You believed
a Higher Power saved you from the drink.

O gods, oh Higher Power,
Let him live. Let her
live! Win this wager,
this pile of red beans.

This from the petitioner
on the pier, who, like
that other maternal progenitor,
Marjorie,
fears.

Marjorie who wanted
to be good,
as she,
and often wasn't,
as she…

Who thinks now
you are too far away
to hear this conjuration,
Not to mention that
you are presently
comprised of only a
few cells.

So do the mental exercise again
again
The spaces
The spaces
where the god intrudes.

MARKINGS

When she first came to me
out of the woods, where
she begged food
from campers to feed herself
to feed her kittens,

She'd look at me
out of round eyes,
as if to ask me can it be?
This daily bowl set down.
For me?

Then she would
come into my bed,
and wet me.
Warm
I'd feel it, then,
the feral reek.

I'd cry out and
slap,
Until I sensed
that it was love she offered,
and gratitude

Possessing me.
If she were possibly—behind the face
that all cats have—extraordinary,
gifted,
She would have written poems
on my body,
 pop songs:
"Sea of Love…"

But gifted
or no, all she could offer
was her warm urine.

That is past. She eats now
out of little golden cans, and stares
unblinking on her
good fortune,
Expressed lately by sudden
leaps up to the mantle
and little fantasies of chase

up stairs and
over couches.

What causes me to think of this today is
a small memorial, the bottom of my hill,
where I walk mornings, where
a motorcyclist, following too fast
a curve of road
that follows a curve of river,
smashed himself
against a tree.

To the tree are pinned, fresh
each week, offerings of poems,
letters, foil balloons and
plastic flowers…

It must all be expressed
somehow, I'm thinking,
scratched in caves, spray painted
on derelict walls and overpasses…what?
Our pain, our love,
excreted, scrawled.

MONARCH

Sitting at the kitchen window, she sees a Monarch
flitter by; seems years since she has seen one
On the phone she hears him saying something,
sounds like moustache, tries to figure out
who's called him...missed beginning of his sentence,
mind flown out the window where
Monarch hovers over pink Impatience.

They'll die tonight, according to the antic
weatherman: a mass of frigid air from Canada is
moving in to blacken annuals of the tender sort...
She loves the tender annuals, after all those years
of living on the Equator, seeing nothing
but the waxy, florid perennials...

Place of seasons brought by a moist eddy of winds
returning with their burden of monsoon.
Nothing to do with the tremendous cranking over
of the Earth's entire axis.

...this girl.
I saw her in a dream,

he's saying.
Who is he talking to?
He has no friends...
He used to have so many...well not so many, but a few
good... Now, he has none she knows of.

Just this almost man who calls him sometimes...

She doesn't know his name.

...and there she's sitting next to me at the office
of the Freudian Shit...
he says.

She makes him see the Freudian Shit.
To her he's just
a mild man who
apologizes too much.
She hasn't
that much faith in him.

...same girl I saw in my dream the night before.
But who would listen to this stuff?

she wonders.

Perhaps that boy he got in trouble with once...Tim...
They shot an arrow once
into the steeple of the Congregational Church...
A weak boy, let himself be dominated;
but even he, she hasn't seen around...

She went to see the mother, found her
in her nightgown four-thirty in the afternoon
sitting at the kitchen table with a pound of coffeecake
she's sharing with the children's pony.
She's brought the pony in the kitchen
for company.

I'm depress éd, she'd said.
They'd laughed.
She liked her, though she didn't approve of things
she did, like going out Ricard's Farm
to steal pie apples...
This woman liked to shop lift too.
It gave her life an edge, she said.

She also liked provoking the town's historic
commission—these were the people in charge of nothing
ever changing—by painting her old house
in violent uncolonial colors.

Her origins were South Boston, they suspected,
and they weren't far from wrong.
Her father, a coal dealer
from Melrose.

It wasn't easy being town's sole
representative of the Melrose Irish.
Of the lower middle class...

And she was intelligent, and even
the jarring colors tasteful in a way, invoking
Salem witches, black and pumpkin colors...

She wrote all her children's essays,
won a contest once, for fifth graders.
She even wrote a three page letter to her
husband once, beseeching him to ascend the
cellar stairs for supper.

A unique reaction, hers,
to suburban boredom.

They laughed a lot and had a glass of sherry
after two. They counted minutes until two.

Another thing, her Timmy liked to fiddle.
Once he asked to use her phone and fiddled it into
forty pieces on the coffee table.

He did the same thing to the public phones
outside the Ethical Society, and
there was the matter of the arrow in the
steeple of the Congregational Church,
but it was all boy mischief.

They could laugh.
She hadn't laughed awhile, since
last she had a friend, and so did he.

This person on the phone, however,
is something other...

The Monarch's tiny flame, she thinks, will flicker down
a continent to that pass they used to take when they
were going to the beach at Cata, high rain forest
where a mythic dictator built a gloomy dormitory
for scientists to lie in wait for Monarchs.

Once she saw a mountain lion cross the dripping road,
as they were dropping in their Volkswagen filled with
picnic baskets, through strata of eucalyptus, then
and coco palms, to the blue Caribbean.

So when you gonna bring me stuff you told me
gives me dreams? he says, and she
takes the stuff that gives her dreams from
underneath the kitchen cupboard.

A mass of Canadian air means a lengthy absence
of impatient impatience and butterflies,
long shadow over this New England. Slow passing,
yes, eternity of absence; and, like
the antic weatherman, she won't commit
herself as to their coming back...

WE THOUGHT IT WOULD NEVER...

Oh it was hilarious. That time we had The Storm. And had no heat Or lights and had to camp on Laurie's sofas. with borrowed blankets. And had that argument about Bill Clinton's statement:
"I did not have sexual intercourse with That Woman."

Oh it was...We thought it would never...

He wasn't lying I said. You were both Appalled. No, you're both too Young I said, To remember those days. Sexual intercourse was something Got you pregnant.
You had to put it in the proper place.

Lying about on our sofas—We had become territorial about our sofas—
Heavy petting it was called then I declared.

David had walked to Seven Eleven. Bought us coffee. There was a ship washed up
Across the highway, we were told. No lights anywhere, except for here. The little neighborhood on the other side of the river where that Seven Eleven had a block long line outside.

Snooky had lost her home. She was up in a helicopter On TV Viewing that jumbled
Disassembled Party House. Where there was once such Hilarity.
Oh it is too funny.

In the kitchen cooking Something sodden from my freezer or David's austere cupboard.
Some brown rice turned by microwaves into a brick. Might be used, I said for some craft project...

A friend calls from another state. I know you're near the bay...
But High I say. My house is high. And the two on the sofas laughing. My house is high I tell her
And I am high. Oh it was so hilarious. We thought it would never...

But all the time, you Laurie, the proprietor of the sofas were awaiting that trip to
Sloan Kettering. And David bravely drove us. All three. The trip through the tunnel required Three in the car---they counted. Absurdly, pulling us over. Oh everything was so absurd....

We went in as a family. Three people who had only recently met, to face the severe doctor
who offered a risky transplant and 50/50 chances...

After, only one restaurant had food. Gyros.
David, who was grieving a breakup with a Mexican waiter he loved, sat opposite with his overgrown curls and his sweet smile.
And I said, seeking to console him, You're so good looking David.
Laurie and I could really go for you.
He doesn't smile. Looks abashed.
Bad joke.
And Laurie silent, thinking of that 50/50 Chance.
Oh I was cruel.

Cruel in my wanting to keep aloft that levity, that laughter. And Oh, it was so hilarious and Bill Clinton wasn't lying and we thought it...
We thought it would never
We thought it would
Never end...

Barbara de la Cuesta has been past recipient of fellowships in fiction from the Massachusetts Artists' Foundation, and the New Jersey Council on the Arts, as well as residencies at the Ragdale Foundation, The Virginia Center, and the Millay Colony. Her poetry collection, *Rosamundo*, was published in 2017 by Finishing Line Press. Her novel, *The Spanish Teacher*, was winner of the Gival Press Novel Prize in 2007, and a more recent novel, *Rosa* was winner of the Driftless Novella Prize from BrainMill Press, in 2017.

www.ingramcontent.com/pod-product-compliance
Lightning Source LLC
LaVergne TN
LVHW041602070426
835507LV00011B/1268